MAKING THINGS SPECIAL

The Art of User Experience Design

Book No. 2

by Hillel Cooperman & Jenny Lam

Edited by Scott Berkun
Illustrated by Tom Chang

JACKSON FISH MARKET PUBLISHING

Jackson Fish Market Publishing

1425 Broadway #448

Seattle, WA 98122

www.jacksonfish.com

Ordering Information: Quantity sales. Special discounts are available on quantity purchases by corporations, associations, and others. For details, contact Jackson Fish Market Publishing at (206) 724-4144 or visit www.makingthingsspecial.com.

Printed in the United States of America

Publisher's Cataloging-in-Publication data

Cooperman, Hillel; Lam, Jenny.

Making Things Special : The Art of User Experience Design / Hillel Cooperman and Jenny Lam.

Typeset in Minion Pro – an Adobe Original typeface by Robert Slimbach, Whitney by Hoefler & Co., and Helsing by Great Lakes Lettering.

p. cm.

ISBN 978-1-945308-50-5

1. The main category of the book —Design —Business. 2. Art

First Edition

14 13 12 11 10 / 10 9 8 7 6 5 4 3 2 1

CONTENTS

Making Things Special: The Art of User Experience Design

PREFACE

Hi. Welcome to our second book. :)

In our first book, Tech Leadership from the Trenches, we spent our time talking about how designers and design-savvy folks could navigate and direct their organizational structures to create great user experiences. In this book we get down to the next level of detail. How do we identify our target audience? How do we talk to our customer? How do we avoid getting distracted along the path? How do we make something that stands out? How do we create beauty? What should our values be on this shared journey? These are just a few of the questions we try and tackle in this volume of Making Things Special.

As always, these are just our ideas, based on the humbling experience of trying to create user experiences that we're proud of. As with any creative endeavor, there's always room for differing perspectives, critique, and alternate approaches. We welcome the discussion, and hope you'll our contribution will spark you into creating something that you're proud of.

Hillel Cooperman
hillel@jacksonfish.com

Jenny Lam
jenny@jacksonfish.com

CHAPTER ONE

Who's Your Customer?

In the left-brained world of software development all problems are nails, and logic and reason are the hammer. It goes something like this:

> *We're building a new piece of software. We should understand who it's for so we can build the thing they want. How can you know what to build if you don't understand the person you're building it for?*

And in essence, this is correct. Knowing the needs of the audience whose problem you're trying to solve can be a big help in building the right experience. But therein lies the rub. When understanding the dreams, motivations, and fears of human beings that are not ourselves, our tools are woefully crude. More often than not, whatever tidbits we do glean about our audience are just that, scraps and fragments. Certainly not a complete picture. Even worse, we don't know how to weigh these factoids, and we have essentially no idea how large the space is that remains undefined.

But in the business world, where people are clamoring for logic and reason as the basis for decisions, people typically will base their decisions on the data they have, even if that data only represents a tiny fraction of the overall picture.

Is optimizing around a few datapoints out of hundreds or thousands any better than flying blind?

Matters get even more complicated as the value of technology is no longer just about its functionality but also about the emotional connection it makes with customers. Worrying about an emotional connection is usually reserved for products of the arts. But software too is now subjected to this dimension. Who is the target customer for the TV show 30 Rock? Would having a demographic profile of the average audience member help the writers make it funnier? More interesting? Would the creators of the program have been helped by speculating about their target audience in advance of their first episode? Possibly creating a mock persona of the 30 Rock audience member? This is not to say that there aren't traits that are common across the show's viewers — mostly their appreciation of Tina Fey's sense of humor. It's just that the audience's shared characteristics seem unlikely to help its creators make a better experience.

Here's the difficult truth. The customer for your new piece of software is… YOU.

It has to be. There's no other person you can know. There's no other person for whose feelings you can really intuit, their dreams, what makes them tick.

Once a product exists, once a product is in production, then you can shed your burden. Then you have real customers. You can find out who they are. You can watch them use your product. You can ask them questions. But until your software is in use, by real people, in non-contrived environments, the customer is you. Whether there are other people who share your feelings and values about the product your building, and will pay to user it, is another matter entirely.

But for new products, new categories, rather than basing your design around the smattering of datapoints you can measure in an opaque sea of unmeasurable traits, our suggestion is to create something for yourself. Embracing humility and wallowing in customer data can come once you've got something out in the wild.

CHAPTER TWO

Software is a Conversation

Software is a conversation between the designer and the user. And historically, the designer talking to you when you use most software is a passive aggressive jerk.

Let's take one simple example, found on thousands of forms across the world wide web – the submit button. SUBMIT! How does that make you feel? Is the software talking to the user? Is the user talking to the software? Is barking out a terse 'submit' ever a nice thing to say?

Confusingly, language is both powerful and weak in user experience design. Google built its ad business based on text advertisements, not the flashier graphically heavy display advertising. Good headlines on blog posts make all the difference in the world when it comes to enticing someone to click. And yet, we know that most of the text found in software user interfaces simply isn't read. Users are perpetually scanning, skimming, and jumping around trying to do the least work possible to understand how to accomplish their goal.

The traditional thinking says:

> *A concept is hard to explain to the user with only a self-evident user interface? No problem, just put it in the user manual. And as for the user... RTFM!*
>
> *But...*
>
> *...manuals are now extinct. So when we have something that's hard to explain, how about putting in a bunch of explanatory text? The user will read the text in the actual user interface and then understand the complexity of the software.*

But we know users won't read it, and will be confused, so what is the answer?

The answer is the respectful helper.

The baseline voice to start with is that of someone friendly, but not overly familiar, and ultimately there to serve – an incredible server at your favorite restaurant perhaps? There when you need them, gone when you don't. Not intruding, but definitely putting you at ease. Efficient in language — definitely not verbose. And ultimately focused on serving the user effectively without being overly familiar or chummy.

Some thoughts on language in software:

Coherence. Your tone needs to carry throughout the experience. On your website, in your app, when someone talks to tech support, in the marketing materials, and even when watching a demo at the trade show booth (or whatever it is people do instead of trade shows these days). Your software, your company needs one voice. One coherent voice. If the ads speak in one voice, and the product in another, your customers will experience the cognitive dissonance of realizing their date doesn't look like the picture in the person's dating site profile. Nobody wants that.

Friendliness. Walk the line between informal and overly familiar. There's no need for ma'ams and sirs when it comes to software text. But, being too friendly makes people uncomfortable. And ultimately, software is someone you work with — occasionally, not a member of your family or a boss. Say please and thank you. And please note, none of this implies a specific type of personality. You can be formal friendly or casual friendly. It's not just fine, but encouraged to understand the tone of voice you should be using with your users based on your overall brand values.

Brevity. Your users don't read. And even when they do, they don't comprehend. Not because they lack reading comprehensions skills, but because they have better things to do than read your essays explaining the complexity of your software. If you need to "explain" something with a paragraph of text in the user interface, you've already lost. The less text on the screen, the more chance they'll read what remains. Edit. Edit. Edit.

Testing. Test that text. When it comes to driving users to act, there's really no better way to know what users will respond to than testing a few options. Each headline, subject line, link text, text ad, can all be tested. Whichever drives the most customers to take the action (and be happy they took it) is the right one. Some people are better than others at writing text that drives action, but nobody is a perfect predictor. Testing trumps all on this one.

If all this is too much, do this simple test. When you write a piece of text for your user interface, say it aloud, to another person. Are they annoyed? Do they want to punch you? Are their eyes glazing over? If so then you need to rewrite that text or get rid of it entirely. In fact, let's summarize this entire piece of advice. To paraphrase a famous Rabbi out of context, when it comes to using language in software user experiences, "that which is hateful to you, do not do to your user."

hello

CHAPTER THREE

Less is more - and here's why.

One of the secret advantages of making software today is the ability to ship that software to real customers early and often. Those users are a treasure trove of feedback helping you find your way through the fog of software development. You can listen to their compliments and complaints as well as watch how they actually do and don't use the product. And you get to constantly refine your plans as a result.

But there is one thing that can get in your way — not shipping often enough. Not shipping is kryptonite to making customer feedback a regular part of your process. We often say that constraints force creativity. Constraints also force clarity.

> *"If I had more time, I would have written you a shorter letter."*
> *–Blaise Pascal*

Your job as the product design leader is the find the one thing — the single thing your product needs to do well. Some people call it the minimal viable product. Some people call it your main scenario. Call it what you like, but it is the one thing you will deliver in v1. And within that scenario you will further constrain your investment to the fewest components that make your delivery distinctive.

It is common for professional technologists to fret over not having enough features. "If features 1-3 don't get everyone excited, shouldn't we add features 4 and 5?" It's human nature to want to maximize your chances for success. The thinking goes as follows: the more stuff you put in there, the more opportunity you have to resonate with a customer. But this model breaks down quickly. Think of a delicious and unassuming pizza. Let's keep it simple and just put pepperoni on it. But what about people who don't like pepperoni? Let's add anchovies. And for vegetarians? How about pineapple? How many people will want a pepperoni/anchovy/pineapple pizza? Some maybe, but not many.

But even worse than turning off your customers with things they don't need or want is the distracting those customers from understanding the core of who you are. If you're going to make an incredible pizza — certainly a crowded market — you better make sure your simple cheese pizza is fantastic. No toppings are necessary to make it clear that your pizza beats every other pizzeria in town. If you can't create that baseline and make an impression, then you've already failed and no amount of toppings will save the day. In fact, the toppings just add confusion and distraction from your identity and your core value.

And let's say that your base pizza was in fact amazing, but your anchovies were subpar. The more complexity you added to your pizza, the harder it is to discern what people liked and didn't like. While the anchovies were the issue we might think it was the pepperoni, or the pineapple, the sauce, the cheese, the crust, etc. Teasing apart the whys and wherefores of customers' negative (and positive) reactions can be challenging. The simpler you keep it the better.

And finally, what if you had to invest in a new slicer to get your pepperoni just the right thickness, but it turns out that your customers don't like pepperoni. You didn't just cloud your customers impression of your product, but you now have infrastructure investments and cost sunk into functionality that you really didn't need in the first place.

Find the one impactful thing. Do it well. And then, with each successive release you get to add little bits here and there and see how customers respond. Maybe this week we'll do a sausage special. If it sells well, maybe we'll incorporate it into the permanent rotation. If the sausage required special infrastructure (a special sausage-making machine?), maybe we'll do it manually to start because we're not sure it's gonna be a hit. Once it's a hit we can invest in the special sausage-making equipment. You get the idea.

In addition to learning about delivering less to your customers you've now also learned a bonus lesson: pizza analogies are almost always useful in illustrating important concepts.

Now that you understand the importance of giving the spotlight to that one important piece of functionality, in the next chapter we'll talk about how to figure out what to put there.

CHAPTER FOUR

One Thing

Just because something is said often, attaining the status of cliché, doesn't mean it's not true. Clichés however are defined as trite or without substance. Allow us to make sure that this phrase is neither.

Do one thing, and do it well.

This may sound easy. This may sound simple. It's not. When it comes to the "ease" with which things are done well, in our experience, it only looks easy. In reality it's an impressive amount of effort, thought, and often repetitive and difficult work that does something "well". Allow us a moment to take an example from the culinary world.

One of our favorite soups is fresh summer corn soup. A corn soup where every spoonful tastes like you just bit into a fresh cob of corn picked right off the stalk. Not even cooked in terms of the freshness of the flavor (if not the texture). How hard could it be to make that soup? Turns out it's not so simple. First you need to pick high quality corn. If you don't have the right core ingredients, no amount of seasoning will save your soup. Then you're going to shave off all the niblets from the cobs and sauté them gently. Perhaps it will just be olive oil and a little salt. Or perhaps you'll use some sort of cured cut of pork to provide your salt and fat. Once the niblets start to release their flavor, you'll add just enough water to cover them in the pot. You'll cook them until they turn to mush — all the while seasoning as appropriate.

Once you've cooked the hell out of your corn, without letting it get brown, you'll take it off the heat and let it cool. Once cool, you'll use hand blender to get a better consistency. More soup like. In fact, what you're making is essentially a simplified veloute. It's that "velvety" consistency you're going for. But the hand blender won't be enough to get there. Now you're going to push your veloute through a tamis (a super fine grain mesh) to eliminate any pulp or chunks above a certain size. Now if you've done your job properly, what's left is a gorgeous, silky, pale yellow, simple thickish soup bursting with the essential flavors of the original niblets that were attached to their cob just an hour earlier. You can serve it hot or cold. And in either case the diner's mouth should burst with the essence of summer on each spoonful.

Why have we taken this jaunt into the kitchen? Because this soup is a perfect example of doing one thing, and doing it well. Here's what we really did:

- We focused. We picked corn. We didn't hedge our bets and say corn AND tomatoes, or corn AND sausage. Just corn. This takes courage. This takes a recognition that corn alone isn't boring. It's exciting. It's that signal that summer is happening and you are experiencing it. Making a choice like this is harder than it looks.

- We believed in the core value of our main ingredient. We could have "thickened" our flavor profile with chicken stock, or added to our texture with cream or egg. But we didn't. We bet that the corn, salt, oil, water combination prepared slowly, patiently, and in just the right combination with just the right core ingredients would yield something that diners fell in love with.

- We didn't add stuff. Even if you have the courage to pick one focus for your creation, it's hard not to try and stuff the dish with supporting characters in case the corn alone seems somehow too simple, too lonely. We could have made corn and piquillo pepper soup, or corn with black truffle soup, or chicken noodle corn soup, or corn soup with vanilla balsamic whipping cream. And while many of those sound delicious, and may in fact be lovely dishes in the long term, right now we're just trying to get our corn soup right. Adding those "enhancements" are only likely to distract us from the foundation of our dish. If we've done our job right, then the corn soup alone will be so wonderful, it won't need supporting characters.

And here's the most important magical result of this type of approach: only once we learn how to make that corn soup so fantastic that it doesn't need any supporting ingredients, that is the first moment where we're truly able to:

- know what's involved in making each ingredient to that incredible high standard.

- have a foundation for our dish that is good enough to stand on its own

- have a deep sense for the flavor profile of that foundation which will inform which supporting ingredients will truly complement the dish as opposed to take away from it.

Isn't that crazy? It's only once we make the simplest form of the creation, that we have the knowledge, vision, and understanding to add components that enhance it. Today, most people creating consumer experiences – from soup to software – are so busy throwing more junk at their consumer that they never take the time to make sure the absolute core of the experience could stand on its own perfectly.

You may think that this formula for focus is great for consumer focused hyper-simple mobile apps, but inappropriate for your real estate tax management software. Not true. Whether users are engaging in more "consumery" tasks like sharing photos or more difficult and complex tasks like dealing with the IRS, they have a goal and they want to get from point A to point B not only as efficiently as possible but feeling as good as possible at the end of the experience.

Handling taxes on real estate holdings may not feel like a mouthful of summer sunshine, but it could feel at the end like you just completed your task incredibly efficiently and competently, and maybe even saved you time and money that could have gone to the IRS.

But what if people don't end up liking your corn soup? Well, if you can look yourself in the mirror and say you delivered the best possible corn soup, and they still didn't like it, then your audience is not as excited about corn soup as you thought they would be, and no number of adornments (bacon? cherry tomatoes? prawns?) will make up for the fact that the core of your experience is not compelling. Time to pick a new core ingredient. Pattypan squash perhaps?

In our experience, more often than not, successful technologists are not necessarily great at picking the right core ingredient, they're just great at not giving up. They try ingredient after ingredient until they find the one thing that resonates. And only then is it time to add the bacon.

CHAPTER FIVE

Iterative Loops in User Experience Design (or The Death of the Written User Interface Spec)

We do this all the time in life. We start with a broad idea and narrow it down. It's natural. It's normal. It's healthy.

"Want to go out? Food or a movie? What type of food? Which restaurant? What night? What time? Where will we meet? What should we order? etc."

And yet, when we have larger teams, we often try to pathologically plan things out in advance in way too much detail. Now, we know that many teams have taken a much more agile approach over the past few years. But many teams haven't. And it's usually the larger tech teams, where lots of people are working on a project, and managers have been put in place that suffer from the disease that is the illusion that they can plan innovation and creativity.

So how do we iterate and make change in a software development process? We call it, the loop.

Think of a reverse spiral, where with each loop we get closer to the center… we get closer to detail and ultimately to reality. At the outside of the spiral we're just talking and brainstorming. Then we're sketching on whiteboards. Then we're drawing wireframes — maybe with little hints about how the software should function in certain cases. In the meantime, maybe we're experimenting with visual collages to come up with an aesthetic.

We narrow it down to one visual direction. Then we're drawing a set of visual elements that look like user interface elements. We're experimenting with color. At some point the visual language feels coherent, and the wireframes are telling a story of the software's interaction. Next, we're applying the visual language to some subset of the wireframes – they look like real user interface screens. We know how the software will feel. In the meantime, the engineers have started coding. Maybe they've focused exclusively on the back end. Or maybe they've built the front end based on the wireframes without a visual treatment knowing they'll apply that on top once it's done. After all, the wireframes should have accurately defined 90% of the elements on screen even though their presentation isn't decided yet.

By this time, the detailed mockups (visual language applied to the wireframes) and the code are ready to engage in a full on slow dance. Holding each other close, tight, and in rhythm. The coders are now implementing the comps in code. And as time marches forward, and we get closer to sharing that software experience with the world… the software is coming to life. It was in our heads, and now it's living and breathing and being touched and succeeding and sometimes failing. And we're tweaking it, and changing it, and pinching here, and tucking there. It's not quite what we imagined back on the whiteboard, but it's somehow, even better. Each loop gets clearer, sharper, and has progressively more detail until the code itself is the sharpest picture that can exist of the experience because it IS the experience. When everyone is focused and excited, the process of revealing this clear picture can feel like magic.

Celebrate the fact that you're creating a software user experience and not a skyscraper. It's the only reason you get to take shortcuts like this.

And these shortcuts, the things that didn't happen, in some ways they are the most critical elements to making this work:

- There were no written "specs". The wireframes and visual design exercise were the closest thing there were to specs. Engineers work directly with user experience designers when there's not enough detail. Either the engineer has enough experience to fill in any missing details in the right way, or the engineer and the designer work it out on the whiteboard as the engineer codes. There are also no testers complaining about the lack of specs. This is possible if the engineers are writing their own tests. The fewer people that work on a part of the product, the fewer people need to know how it works and what the intentions are for the behavior. We've worked on enormous projects where there were detailed specs, meant to be updated with every single change. I'll tell you now… other than possibly in rare cases in software written for the Defense Department, THIS NEVER HAPPENS. The specs never get updated with every detail. And if they're off by a little but, they might as well not exist at that point. Dream all you want, it won't happen.

- Of the spec-like things that were created — wireframes, etc., nobody went back and updated them when changes were made in later stages. Once you agree on a stage that it feels right, the team moves forward. Never backwards. Whatever stage you're in becomes the spec. And finally, the code is the spec. It's the living breathing document that dictates reality. Not some piece of paper, or a sketch.

- Everyone understood that in the early loops there were many details not covered.

And they understood this because they were details that could be determined later. For example: the wireframes must detail the global organization of the app's functionality and what affordances a user will use to switch between those major areas. But the wireframes DO NOT need to detail what happens when a user types in the wrong password. We know what happens. They get an error. Is there room for improvement in the password error experience? Sometimes. At some point do an engineer and a designer need to collaborate to design and execute that experience?

Yes. Can that be done in a sidecar fashion? Yes. You may ask, how do you know which items are important, and which aren't in terms of when they need to be defined in the process? Well, the worst answer we could give is: experienced software creators just know. A better answer is this: for situations where there are tried and true solutions, for situations where the design is encapsulated in the experience and doesn't affect a bunch of other areas, for situations where we're not trying to make this a signature moment of the experience: for these situations, they can probably be deferred to later in the process without much of a ripple effect. We're sorry this answer is so vague. But those of you who've made software before know this.

But the big question is why? Why are the above elements NOT part of the iterative process? The race to create a great user experience, to have a team be in sync about creating something wonderful and define the right details at the right point in the process is a delicate balance. We don't live in a world of unlimited resources. (And even if we did it would only paralyze us from making anything anyway.) We also don't live in a world where people love debating tiny details that should be trusted to small groups. We live in a world where these projects need to exist in a reasonable time frame with quality and distinctiveness. And you must eliminate some of these brittle and constraining tendencies in large project software development in order to make something great. Otherwise you end up with something mediocre delivered in twice the time. And nobody wants that. Not even the government.

~~~

Before you start writing e-mails, and posting criticisms, there are certainly exceptions to the above. But to be clear, they are exceptions. In this chapter we're talking about user experience specifications.
~~~

Not software specifications overall. There are scenarios that software is designed to be a part of that are complicated, technical, and require precision. They are the underpinnings of pieces of software that manage millions of financial transactions. Or software for the department of defense managing nuclear silos. We understand that documenting the way some of this software works isn't just a good idea, it's often mandatory. That said, we still don't believe it's necessary in terms of the user interface elements of most projects. Furthermore, while we know this can't always be done, when a spec seems important, try documenting the process, and not the software. How is the credit card supposed to be processed? What is supposed to happen to the electrical grid when there is a failure? The process, the outcome, these are things that deserve being committed to paper. The user experience can be crafted with a lot more lightweight framework. And the result will be better for it.

CHAPTER SIX

"I've got 99 problems, but one that customers actually run into ain't one."

In the rush to ship your software there endless opportunities to polish, refine, and smooth over rough edges. And yet, at some point, you must finish and put it out for customers. How do you decide which problems to fix and which to save for later?

Here's how it works: When you're trying to launch your new software experience, you need to stay focused on your core scenario. Your core scenario is either something entirely new that nobody's ever done (unlikely and scary), or more likely it's an improvement on a scenario competitors already deliver (badly in your opinion). Their crappy experience is your inspiration. Cool. You carve out a straight line for your users where they can accomplish what they want with beauty and grace using your new product. Love it!

But invariably you will invent new problems. You didn't copy the competition or clone them. You followed your own path. And whether it's some rough text, a confusing layout, or just a concept that's misunderstood, you will find new things that need polishing. Some will jump out immediately as you use the product. But many, in fact — most — will be speculative. You won't have run into them personally (and by now you're too close to the product to have great perspective on this anyway), but someone on your team will start a sentence with the words "I worry that..." leading to doubt and concern.

The problem is that there is no shortage of doubts among designers. Just about every issue brought up may be a problem, but it also might not be. The reliable and efficient way to find out is to ship the product and see what your customers actually have a problem with. You simply can't know out of the list of 99 problems that you can come up with, which five are the real ones. And it's only once they have issues that you should address the problems. The rest should be ignored or deprioritized.

Is inflicting some difficult aspects of your experience a "nice" thing to do to your customers? Not really. But is never shipping a product because you're too busy fixing 94 problems that they won't have a "nice" thing to do? No. In fact, it's suicide. Punting a suspected issue you to the next version of your product is scary. But what you're doing is sending the list of potential issues to the "jury" — your customer base. Believe me, they'll let you know, in a hurry, where they're having issues. And then in that next release you can move quickly to solve those issues.

There are many reasons why 94 of the 99 problems won't be reported by customers, or detected by analytics. Your speculation was wrong. Or customers use the product differently than you thought. Or some other problem stops them from even getting to that point. Or that part of the product was ill-conceived and needs to be scrapped entirely. Whatever the reason, be thankful you didn't waste time fixing problems that customers didn't have issues with. Strangely, customers form impressions of a company not based so much on their first impressions, but on their ongoing interactions with the company and its product. And customers that see a product constantly evolving to address their actual top concerns are customers that fall in love with a product and the company behind it.

CHAPTER SEVEN

Why we (almost) never look at the competition.

Often we get tasked to help a company design a product that has a successful competitor. It's hard not to want to deconstruct what the competitor does, copy all the things that make it successful, and then add your own "special sauce" to your version and hope for the best. Unfortunately, this strategy is also often a recipe for mediocrity. It's usually incredibly difficult to dislodge a competitor with your one tweak to their product.

Copying a competitor is fraught with problems. First, it presumes you know which things in a competitor's design make it successful. It may seem obvious to you (it certainly does to authors of articles deconstructing the success of products that have done well). But you're only seeing part of the picture. The product you see is essentially the tip of the iceberg. Without knowing the decisions that went into why the product is the way it is you may be copying as many bad design decisions as good ones. You are also likely completely unfamiliar with the processes they used to arrive at their decisions. Your processes will be different and invariably generate different results. Even if you copy their product faithfully, what will you do when the environment changes and it's their process that generates success, not a particular implementation at one moment in time? And here's the worst part: when you crib from your competitor, you are basically rudderless, giving them control over YOUR product. Why would you do that?

Products come from people. The DNA that forms teams and groups is very specialized. You need to find the product that can be created honestly from your group's specific cultural genetics – something that your group is passionate about. Anything else isn't genuine. Are you working with a bunch of people who are happy copying someone else's ideas all day? If so, we suggest you find a new group of people to work with as your current co-workers are passionless.

Either you have a genuine vision for making something better than them or you don't. And if you don't, our suggestion is to not bother with the project at all. It's critical to be honest with yourself here. Most people are not good at being introspective on this point. (Our editor has asked us to acknowledge at this point that we've just told you that you need to do something that most people don't have the capacity to do well. He thinks that it's kind of frustrating and pointless. We suppose he's right. The best we can do is apologize, but remind you that we've never believed that all problems have solutions.)

Ultimately, if you're going to create a special product you need to create it based on a vision you have yourself. It can be inspired by other products, but it ultimately must come from a picture in your head, not a picture of someone else's product.

When we're creating products with established competitors we avoid looking at the competition until the vision in our heads is fully formed. We want to be pure and cohesive about what we're building and then check the other guys only when it's time to make sure we've covered our bases. We're not above borrowing stealing great ideas that work. But they need to be the exception and not the rule.

Be yourself. Customers can tell when you're not.

CHAPTER EIGHT

Think Differently

Let's expand on the notion of how we think about competitors.

We were sitting in a room with a client. We were early in the process of trying to create a new and compelling version of their software. The client had multiple established competitors and was trying to expand their reach to new untapped markets.

We came up with what seemed like a novel way to execute a particular feature and the client said this:

> "I don't like that."
>
> We responded, "why not?"
>
> "It's weird."
>
> "Weird?"
>
> "Nobody else does it that way."
>
> "So?"
>
> "So we shouldn't either."

Before we dive in on this topic, let's just say that when you are pioneering new scenarios that have never been served by a product, you're probably thinking differently enough. But in many cases, when you're delivering something that other people have done, you've got to carefully consider this fork in the road – *should you try to distinguish yourself by delivering the feature in a different way OR should you do what everyone else does?*

When we explored this issue with the client, they assumed that if all their competitors were doing it a certain way, that it must be right. But this wasn't clear to us. How did the client know their competitor's engagement rates on this particular feature? They didn't. How did the client know what alternatives had been explored? They didn't. How did the client know that the competitors even measured the effectiveness of this particular feature or that this feature was important to their competitor's customers? They didn't.

Assuming that just because someone's product does things a certain way, that it should be copied often entails a dangerous set of assumptions. In our experience, even if you worked at the competitor you often would not have the data to know whether the decision was the right one or not, so assuming you have enough data when you don't work there seems ludicrous.

So what are the criteria to decide when to be different? Good question!

The first fork in the road is to decide if this feature is a signature moment in our product. Is it core? Is it one of those basic elements on which the whole experience rests? If the answer is yes, we believe that not only should you consider doing something different, unless you can make a compelling case otherwise, you should assume that something different is required.

Being different is what makes you stand out. Being different when it counts is how you make sure that your unique qualities get noticed.

If however, the functionality is not core to the experience, and has established UX patterns that have been tested and proven, then the bar gets dramatically higher for doing something different. Best to stick with an established pattern unless you can make some serious improvements.

In the end, think of this as a resource question. Do you want to spend your time reworking the "change password" functionality or investing in the new whiz bang functionality that defines your entire product and will blow people away?

In the next chapter we'll talk about techniques for making that one feature stand out using the magic of design.

CHAPTER NINE

Standing Out

It used to be enough that a technology existed. It used to be enough that now we could do something we couldn't do before. Whether it was adding up a column of numbers, or WYSIWYG editing of a document, or listening to music, or the web! But creating new categories of software is a hard task. It's happening less and less. And the number of entrants in each category is only increasing. This is the sign of a maturing (and saturated) industry. What to do with the 72nd app in an existing category? How will anyone notice your new to-do list app? Or your amazing new word processing software? Will anyone pay attention to yet another social network?

Have no fear. There is a weapon in your arsenal that you can use to attack this problem. That weapon is design. And don't worry, using the weapon effectively is hard enough that merely knowing that design is the answer is no guarantee that of success.

The key in distinguishing your software experience is expressing focus through design. And the first step is answering the question of "why". Why are you making a new app in this already overpopulated category? What makes you so much better? You don't have to prove that you're better empirically. You don't have to have a longer list of features. What you need to do is believe in your heart that your solution makes the competition look like antiquated garbage, and then convey your belief through the magic of focus and design in your experience.

Does your product do something better than the competitor? Then build your entire identity around that advantage. (e.g. the iPod vs. every other MP3 player in existence when it was launched. And what did the iPod do better? It played music better. It did this by eliminating features and distractions and focusing on the main reason you bought the device in the first place.)

Does your product turn their liability into your advantage? Then lead with that. (e.g. GMail's near unlimited storage vs. the constant hitting of storage limits on Hotmail and Yahoo Mail.)

Does your product simply look ten times better than the competition? (e.g. Flipboard vs. every RSS reader that was out there.)

Let's take a look at Flipboard. Flipboard had less content than the competition, less customization than the competition, ran on fewer platforms than the competition, and yet made the competition look terrible. And even in terms of design, Flipboard had less. A few standard templates, simple clean typography, and one simple animation: the flip. It's not fancy. It's not technically challenging. It's not even necessarily coherent with the visual design. It's just simple and arresting (because nothing else featured this animation so prominently). And yet, the effect is powerful because it is different. And what did Flipboard do? They made it the centerpiece of their identity. It's in their name. They even counted "flips" and claimed it was a meaningful statistic to show off about.

What is the flip? The flip is Flipboard's "signature moment". We'll cover these in detail in another chapter, but you should understand, this simple animation done in the context of all their other focusing decisions makes Flipboard stand out.

Having a hard time knowing how to differentiate yourself? The answer doesn't seem obvious? Examine your most fundamental assumptions. Can any of them be reversed? Can you do the exact opposite of what people expect in one key place?

This doesn't always work, but it's a good method for getting your creative thinking going. Want to make a web encyclopedia that competes with the printed versions? Don't have a huge expensive staff? What if anyone could edit it? Anonymously!

Want to compete with a relatively simple to use blogging platform with millions of users (Blogger)? What if you made a blogging platform that was even simpler (Tumblr)? Or how about one that was even simpler than that (Twitter)? Or how about one that's way more powerful (WordPress)?

There are no right answers here other than to avoid the assumptions that govern the current winner in your category like the plague.

The things that made them successful now constrain their growth. They have an audience that likes their focus. Your job is to come up with a truly different take to peel off users for whom their solution doesn't quite work.

Visual design is another area where you have an opportunity to say something different. And again, some of the best distinctive visual design is a result of the kind of thinking we discussed above. Let's take an example for the consumer products world – Smartfood Popcorn. At the time, retail snacks simply didn't come in black bags. Period. "It just isn't done." When someone utters those words, that's the smell of blood — and you're a shark. It's not that you should recklessly pursue things that aren't done. Because sometimes there are good reasons they're not done. But, often, there's some small notion you can cultivate from those assumptions to help you stand out. Smartfood shipped in a black bag. The world didn't end. People bought it. People ate it. Smartfood succeeded.

Think great visual design needs to be expensive? Take Minecraft or Doodlejump. In an age of videogames costing tens of millions of dollars to produce… In an age where video game graphics look almost like Pixar films. These two games were produced with relatively low-tech graphics. Minecraft went super low-res with pixelated cube graphics representing every object in their world, and Doodlejump was literally that — a bunch of hand-drawn doodles jumping around on your screen. They looked like anyone could have drawn them. Both are hugely successful, both stood out, both were not considered state-of-the-art visual design.

Applying great design in the context of tight focus is what makes things stand out. Getting specific and niche is not a liability, it's a tool to let you distinguish your product in a crowded marketplace.

And don't worry, if you succeed, you can always expand your focus later and become the sprawling all-encompassing market leader that you're now trying to beat.

CHAPTER TEN

Hit it With The Pretty Stick

"Who ever said that pleasure wasn't functional?"
– Charles Eames

Eye candy, lipstick, decoration – that's what a majority of people in the technology industry still think of when they think of aesthetics. When it comes to talking about aesthetics in software, designers and non-designers alike will repeat: "form follows function!" or "whatever works for the target audience!" At this point, everyone politely agrees and the conversation ends. But the question on what makes something beautiful really is never fully put to rest.

Even within the design discipline, the dialogue has changed from visual design as a core design skill to a discussion of defensive denigration of visuals. "Design is about the big "D"!" or "useable over pretty!" – suggesting that aesthetics are superfluous and perhaps the last thing we should concern ourselves with in the product development process. The fact that we don't talk about aesthetics in a formal and consistent way also makes the practice of aesthetics seem like a dark art that's devoid of discipline and subject to the whims of the all-black clad designer. And often those black-clad designers themselves don't dare talk about it should someone think that they're superficial!

Aesthetics are more than just styling and skin. Aesthetics are functional because they communicate and makes us feel. If we strike the right chords in what we communicate and how we make users feel, then our software feels easier to use. If we truly care about making things work for people, aesthetics can't be an afterthought.

Aesthetic's ROI

Why do aesthetics even matter? Other than making us feel some kind of pleasure, does it really have any impact on the bottom line?

Many people will use Mint.com as an example of great design that disrupted the financial product sector and for a good reason. The folks at Mint.com had a user experience vision for managing personal finance and simpler and integrated in a beautiful way. In fact, "make it beautiful" was one of their core product tenets. The Mint.com team made it a beautiful experience first and licensed their tech from Yodlee second. It sold it to Intuit for a lot of money. Was the user interface part of the reason Intiut paid top dollar? A venture capitalist friend of ours was overheard saying, "that right there is $170 million dollars worth of UI." But this is just an anecdote. Let's go to a study.

A study done on the design of Gillette's Venus Razor revealed over the course of a few years that:

> *"For every dollar spent on Advertising, yields $7.21 in increased sales.*
>
> *And for every dollar spent on Aesthetic Design, yields $415.17 in increased sales."**

The aesthetic design they invested in were things like the colors of the razors, the packaging design, the curve of the handle, etc. There is unfortunately not a huge body of academic research on the financial impact of high-quality aesthetics. But feel free to ask your skeptical CEO whether they think design has had any impact on the success of companies like Apple, VW, and Disney?

Aesthetics is the #1 factor in determining site credibility

Mint.com was asking customers to trust the site with all their financial account passwords. That's a huge leap of faith. A huge ask. How do you get people to trust you like that?

According to the Stanford Web Credibility Research center, the number one factor in determining trust is aesthetics. This is the first impression that happens before any reading or other conscious evaluations take place.

> *"Nearly half of all consumers in the study assessed the credibility of sites based in part on the appeal of the overall visual design of the site, including layout, typography, font size and color schemes. ... Beautiful graphic design will not salvage a poorly functioning website. Yet, the study shows a clear link between solid design and site credibility."*

CHAPTER ELEVEN

How to Be Beautiful

We don't see a shortage of people who are making sites that have great content, are usable, and load quickly. Those things are part of design. But even with speed, usability and content in order, the question remains: "is it beautiful?" That's a tough thing to discuss because we can determine if a site is responsive or does it convert users because we have metrics for those things. We don't have a set of metrics to talk about beauty.

First, we'll state the obvious – being great at visual design, or any craft for that matter, takes years and years of practice to get comfortable with the principles, tools, process and the medium. Unfortunately – despite investing all that time you might still be lousy at visual design because there is a healthy amount of raw creative artistic talent needed to for it to come to you intuitively. We're not saying it's absolutely impossible for anyone to become a great visual designer, but it certainly does come easier to some than others.

Unfortunately, there are no hard rules to great aesthetics and there are hundreds of principles. Even if you aren't a great visual designer, there are three fundamental qualities that go into making something aesthetically pleasing:

INTEGRITY, HARMONY, AND RADIANCE

These are what we use in creating and evaluating aesthetics in our day-to-day practice at our user experience design consultancy. We apply these principles to everything from branding to product strategy to user interface, to our advice on improving a customer support phone call.

Integrity

As it relates to product design, Integrity is about the quality of wholeness. About how true, cohesive and about the level of fidelity or quality of a design.

Just think about the car your drive or the knife you use to chop vegetables with. Does it feel like high quality, sturdy, solid? Or does it feel flimsy, weak, unsubstantive? Software can feel like it lacks integrity when there's something about it's presentation layer lacks a position or perspective. When a site doesn't communicate anything or feels generic, it sends out a blank signal that by definition does not ring true. It's not saying anything. Designing and respecting users goals is one thing but pandering to them is another. You can't pretend to be something you're not. At least not forever.

"...you have to stake out what you think is right, put out that signal, make sure it's pure and then do it and know that they will come... But the biggest mistake would be to alter my signal to make sure that I reach all these different people. Because then you're lost."

- Conan O'Brien talking about the entertainment industry

At a micro-level, something as simple as a button having substance and weight can have integrity. Depending on the overall visual style context, a dimensional button can have more integrity than a flat button because it sends a stronger visual affordance.

This is especially true for natural user interfaces with gestural input. It's perhaps why we see a lot more higher fidelity, 3D design in touch applications. The Netflix scrubber control on the iPad is a familiar control for navigating through a timeline of a video but there was great care in the visual design of this particular piece of user interface. The physicality of the circular knob with a generously sized indentation lets me know I can easily control the scrubber with my finger. The large, rounded proportions feel easy and encourages interaction. On top of that, they get bonus points for branding the UI with the Netflix colors and materials which reinforces the brand without beating you over the head with their logo.

But "I'm a minimalist designer"

We hear designers say this a lot and find that it's often used as a crutch when they don't really have anything to say. They don't have an opinion about the visual design. The truth is, really great minimalist design packs a powerful punch because its design has focus. Really great minimalist design is often really difficult to do and doesn't necessarily mean sparse, white, or cold.

So resist the urge to be a faux minimalist. It's boring. We dare you not to boring. Be true. Have something to say. Have integrity.

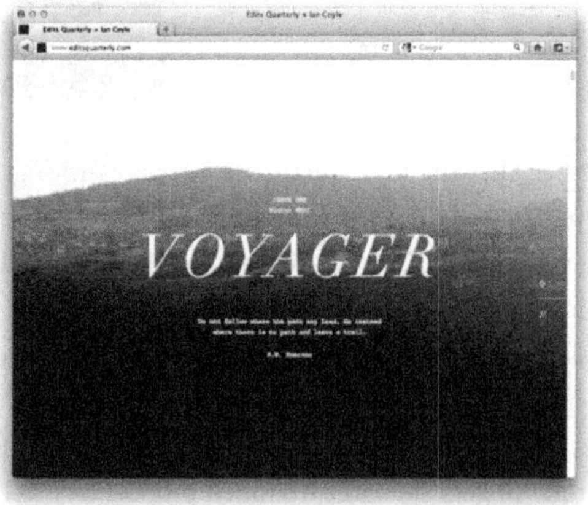

Harmony

Harmony is how the parts relate to the whole. It is similar to the repetition of the round arch and window in the Roman style of architecture; or the recurrence of a common motif in music; the use of a single hue to color the different objects in a painting. All these exemplify aesthetic harmony.

When it comes to visual design, good harmony means that there's a good balance of variation that works with the overall theme. Too many elements, too many textures, can clash creating a chaotic feeling.

Too little variation, no hierarchy, no texture may be harmless but has no visual interest. This becomes a usability issue since everything on the page looks the same so nothing stands out.

Achieving aesthetic harmony isn't only about static elements but also about flow, rhythm, and pacing. The Gutenberg diagram describes a general pattern where the eyes move naturally across a

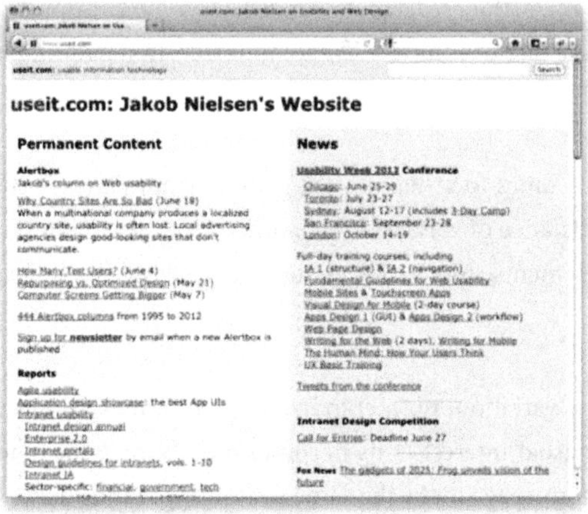

page. Designs that follow the Gutenberg are said to be in harmony with the natural eye flow gravity. These designs can improve rhythm by being in harmony with the natural reading rhythm.

We can't talk about harmony without talking about color. Color is a powerful way of achieving harmony in a design. Often times people get tripped up by choosing color palettes.

A good rule of thumb is to stick to one of these two schemes:

1) Analogous: colors that are adjacent to each other on the color wheel. 2) Complementary: colors are on opposite sides of the color wheel.

It's always a good idea to try to keep the saturation levels and the values (how light or dark a color is) in the same range.

Radiance

The third and final principle is aesthetic radiance. Radiance is the pleasure we feel when we experience a good design. It is at the heart of great aesthetics and something that most software experiences fail at. It's the moment when Instagram makes the user feel like a

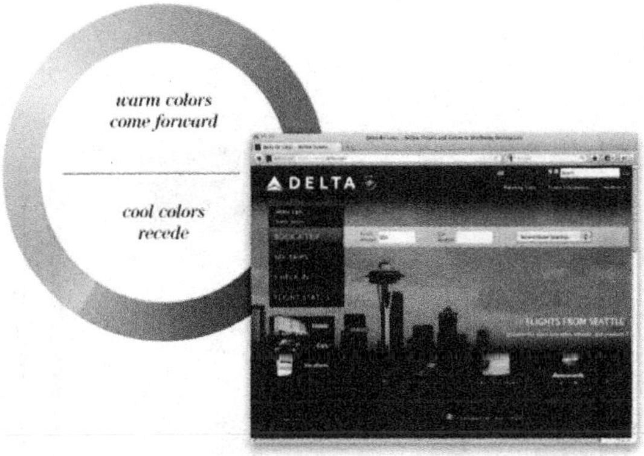

pro photographer by turning your so-so photo into a beautiful image, or it's the surprise music video you get when you complete the Plants vs. Zombies adventure. Achieving radiance has the power to make your product stand out from the competition, increase usage and loyalty, and it has the potential to turn your customers into a sales force.

Aesthetic radiance is hard to describe but there are some design principles that help support it.

Contour Bias

This is the idea that humans favor elements with roundness vs. elements with sharp angles or points. It's easy to go overboard on the contour bias principle. We think of the web 2.0 aesthetic much like the the Reubenesque style of art. Exaggerated proportions and overly-stylized. Art critics refer to this kind of art unsettling and consciously artificial.

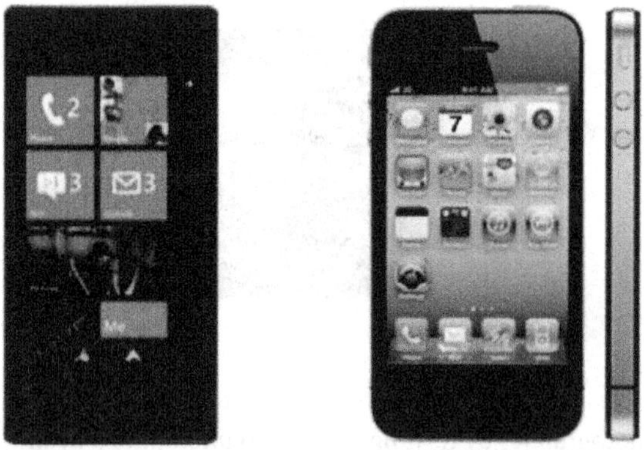

~~~
~~~

Lighting

Lighting is perhaps the most underused visual design device to create radiance. Draining the visuals of color creates strong contrast of light and dark And looking at these examples, it's easy to see what you're supposed to be focused on. Use contrast lighting when you're trying to convey a sense of drama and heighten an emotional effect.

~~~

Shadow

Speaking of light, some of the biggest offenders in poor aesthetics come from carelessly executed drop shadows.
~~~

The dead giveaway that a shadow hasn't been carefully designed, is that we see the same drop shadows on the web as we do in Photoshop's default shadow dialog.

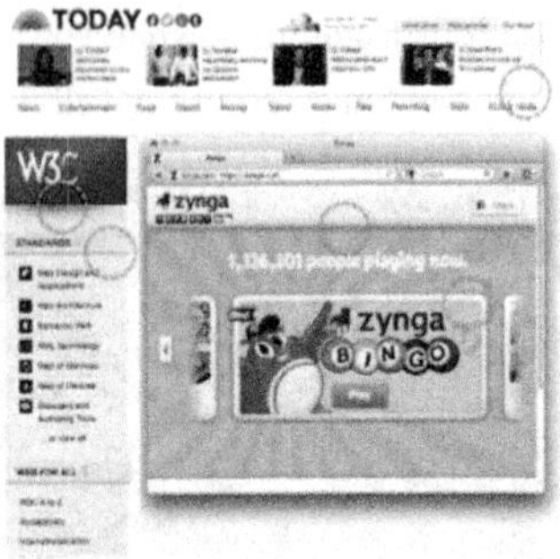

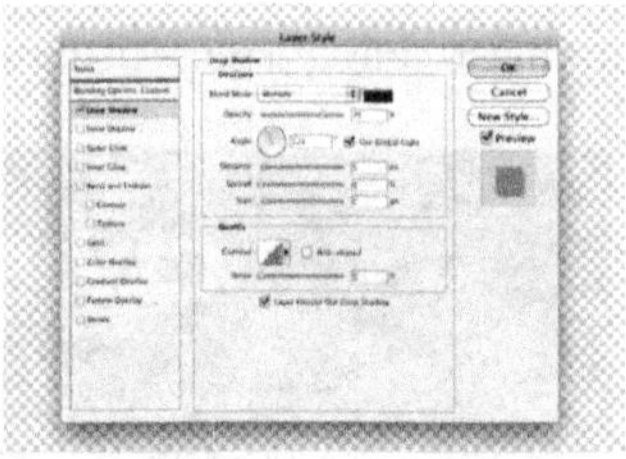

Using lighting, shadows, and gradients to create a sense of dimension is a powerful technique for a UI designer. Thinking about dimension as if you were able to build it in real life can make the design more believable, less confusing, and potentially radiant. When in doubt, keep your shadows subtle and make it human readable.

~~~

Delight

"When one is delighted,
things have the perception of working better."

–Don Norman
~~~

Little details that suprise and delight make people happy. When we're happy, using an interface feels enjoyable and not like a challenge. So when we get confused, we're more likely to explore and find other paths to success. Happy people feel that the product is more usable and desirable.

Check out other great little, big, details here:
http://littlebigdetails.com/

jacksonfish.com's street header image reflects the local time.
Shops would close, street lamps turned on, and moon would come out.

CHAPTER TWELVE

Gratuitous Delight

Utter these two words in a software development meeting and you might get strange looks. But if you think about the moments in any experience that you can actually remember and bring a smile to your face, it's likely those times where the product expresses a little personality, whimsy, and/or empathy.

I remember the first time I ever smiled during a pre-flight security debriefing. It was my first Virgin America flight from Seattle to San Francisco. Instead of awkwardly being forced to watch the flight attendants go through the motions of "teaching" us how to use a seat belt buckle, we were treated to an animated video that poked fun at some of the silly things that travellers have to endure. Everything in the video was on brand. The artsy-sketch aesthetic styling of the animation, the cool tone of the voice-over, the little jokes that empathized with the weary traveller.

These things are not gratuitous. They are deeper expressions of the fundamental spirit of the people behind the products themselves. They serve a purpose – strengthening people's identification with a product and often building their confidence in the team behind it. Above all, delight makes people happy and happy people are more forgiving, more productive and feel that the product is more usable*.

So how do you do this delight thing?

First, we can start with what we know about humans: We're curious, we're lazy, we're highly visual thinkers and learners, we respond to our name and other personal cues like where we live, we find novelty and humor interesting.

If you take these psychological factors into consideration and express them through UI text, a sensory experience like sound and motion, and aesthetically-pleasing imagery all in the spirit of your brand, you create delight.

Brand Delight

The old website for our own design consultancy (Jackson Fish Market) used to feature a street we lovingly called, Jackson Street. It was a row of buildings that represented the products we were shipping or building. The street was a subtle way for people to know what we were up to. Every time we were working on a new product, the scaffolding would go up for one of the storefronts. And by nightfall, Seattle time, the stores would close up shop, the street lights would come on and the moon would shine in the sky.

It wasn't powerful functionality for the site but when people notice it, they love it and they remember us and those little shops.

Signature Brand Moment

Making your product's focus truly special creates a memorable experience that people will tell their friends about. For example, UrbanSpoon app is known for it's usefulness in helping you find the perfect restaurant. But what people remember about it is it's "shake" mode for when you just want UrbanSpoon to help you make the decision. Set a few simple criteria or not and then shake your phone. Jackpot.

Great Conversationalist

One of the most neglected opportunities for getting delight into your UX is in the text. Note the example below from tumblr.com. So easy, so simple, and it doesn't even occupy any additional space. Could you imagine your company having the courage and taking the time to implement this tiny and lovely detail? Let's hope so.

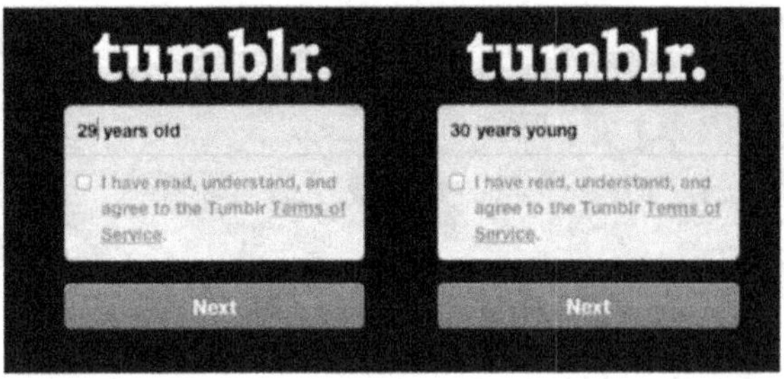

Easter Eggs

"Brains pay attention to what brains care about, not necessarily what the conscious mind cares about. And to the brain, "interesting" is just the most basic prerequisite"

- Kathy Sierra

Humans find pleasant surprises and gifts interesting. Sometimes it's surprising the user with something they didn't think they needed but did or sometimes it's just pleasant unexpected delight.

In Google Maps, if you drop the 3D marker person in Hawaii near the beaches, the avatar is clothed in a hawaiian shirt and surfboard. Relevant and delightful.

You can also look for opportunities in places like footers, background graphics, on hover to provide that extra delight that doesn't get in the way.

Click on the scissors icon three times on Kickstarter.com and it animates across the page and footer falls off. Why? Because it's fun. That's why.

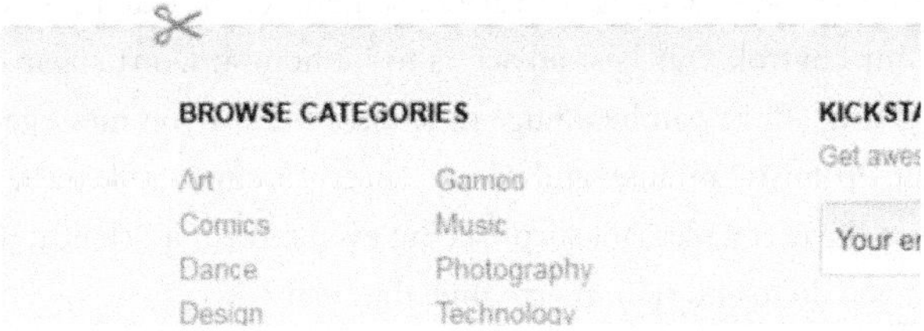

Need a little hint for that problem you're trying to solve on Wolfram Alpha? Just hover over the corner to peel back contextual results.

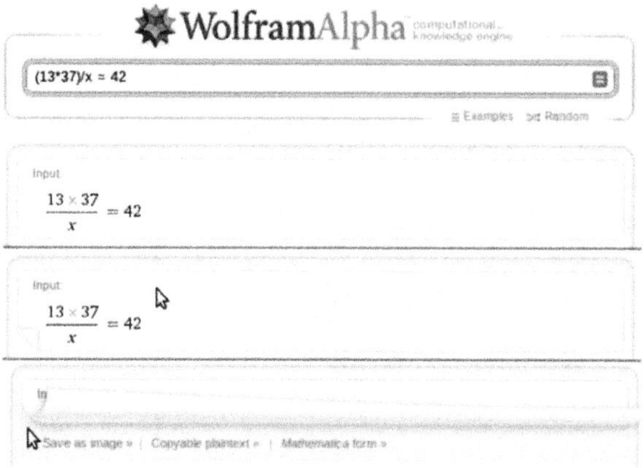

Entertain them while they wait

Unfortunately, people are faced with the problem of waiting for a computer to finish a task relatively often. Whether we're launching an app, buffering a video, loading data, that spinning circle that seems to go on forever. We end up losing our user's attention and they "change the channel".

This moment of delay is critical and sometimes the load time is out of our control. Our best advice is to be honest. Don't sugar coat anything. There can be a huge difference in how you message the wait. Promise 2 minutes and it only takes 30 seconds and you've just given the user a pleasant surprise. But even more importantly, what can you do to entertain them while they wait?

The outer doors on elevators are often surfaced with a reflective material. What better way to pass the time than to examine ourselves in the mirror? Seriously. That's the reason. It makes the time pass easier.

Dropbox does a great job at this with their sync indicator. They have no way of knowing exactly how long it will take but they've delivered this message in a way that is helpful and fun.

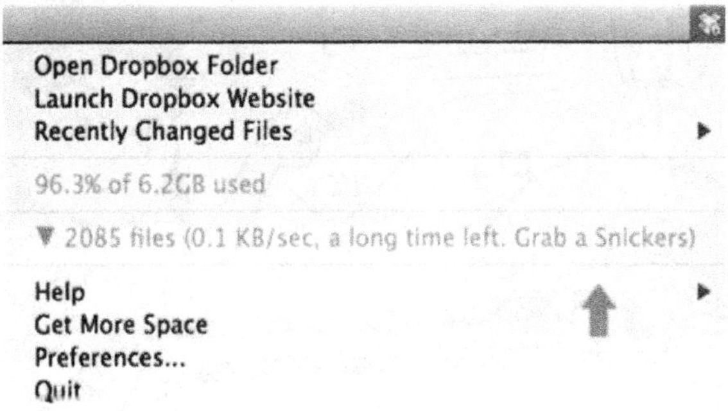

Opportunities:

- the focus of your product language everywhere
- login screen or onboarding experience
- while loading something, entertain them backgrounds, footer, on the periphery transitional moments
- error or dead end (be humble!)
- local culture relevancy (google maps hawaii shirt guy)

1

CHAPTER THIRTEEN

Software Blasphemy – Doing Things Manually

The hallmark of the software professional is that they see a world where technology has an infinite capacity to improve our lives. Software can't put food on a plate, but it can help calculate the most efficient way to grow and distribute the food. Software can't give us a hug (yet), but it can put us in touch with our loved ones. So when you're building new software or new functionality for software it's an opportunity to automate all kinds of things that used to be difficult and arduous processes.

Except, that's not always the case.

Here's an example: A service we worked on had the ability to sell digital content a la carte or as a subscription. Originally the service was designed to sell only a la carte. And that process was automated completely. But when we wanted to experiment with a subscription it was a significant amount of engineering work to make it happen.

We made the investment that let users pay once and consume unlimited content. But the payment processing work was not done and we wanted to try it out. Originally we thought of this as a compromise, but we realized later this was in fact a boon. Why invest significant time in automating the commerce for subscription purchase if the subscription experiment was a failure. We were able to do the bare minimum of engineering investment to find out what customers wanted. And only after determining that subscriptions made sense to our audience did we need to convert our manual/human-driven fulfillment process to a digital one.

This is the kind of step that's often missing at tech companies. After all, why do something manually when code can be written to automate the process? Of course, what's not considered in this calculation is: the likelihood that the functionality will actually be used, the cost to test, update, and maintain the code, the potential churn to other parts of the codebase, and how those latter two costs go up if the experiment turns out to be a bust.

The silver lining of doing a process manually for awhile is that you end up with a much tighter and more solid design of the functionality eventually to be enshrined in code. Actually walking through the commerce process let us know what was actually necessary when writing the code for the functionality. Typically when you design features you're guessing. It's often educated guessing, but guessing nonetheless. Now we knew exactly what the functionality needed to do because we'd done it ourselves, by hand.

CHAPTER FOURTEEN

User Interface Basics

There are numerous excellent books on the topic of user experience design. There are even more on the topic of visual design and brand. We are not going to be able to either exceed the quality of those books in our modest effort, or condense their value into our book. You should know these things. They are the basics, the rules, the structure of the disciplines involved in designing great user experiences. And we don't cover them comprehensively in this series because they've already been covered so well elsewhere.

Here are our recommendations:

- The Design of Everyday Things, Donald A. Norman
- Understanding Comics, Scott McCloud
- Art & Fear, by David Bayles, and Ted Orland

Continued reading list:

- Universal Design Principles, J. Butler, K.Holden, W. Lidwell
- About Face, Alan Cooper
- Simplicity, John Maeda
- Responsive Web Design, Ethan Marcottte
- The Elements of Typographic Style, Robert Bringhurst
- Hooked: How to build Habit-Forming Products, Nir Eyal
- Designing for the Digital Age, Kim Goodwin
- Living with Complexity, Donald A. Norman
- Steve Jobs, Walter Isaacson
- Design Is the Problem, Nathan Shedroff
- Creativity, Inc., Ed Catmull and Amy Wallace
- Seductive Interaction Design: Creating Playful, Fun, and Effective User Experiences, Stephen P. Anderson
- Don't Make Me Think, Steve Krug
- Design, Form, and Chaos, Paul Rand

- Designing Brand Identity, Alina Wheeler
- Interaction of Color, Josef Albers
- The Shape of Design, Frank Chimero
- Designing with Web Standards, Jeffrey Zeldman
- Stop Stealing Sheep & Find Out How Type Works, Eric Spiekerman

CHAPTER FIFTEEN

Intuitive doesn't mean instantly understandable.

> *Note: We know that we recommended that you get the meat and potatoes of user experience design from other books. And that's true, you should. And we said we wouldn't cover those in our book. And in general, we don't. But we snuck in one chapter on meat and potatoes. This one. Because, well, we couldn't resist, and we think it's an important perspective to have as you consider the basics of our craft.*

Human beings learn with all their senses. When it comes to decoding a user experience, we can only rely on sight, sound, and touch. But for some reason, many tech folks these days believe that if a user can't understand your user interface instantly and completely from sight alone then you've failed to make your user interface intuitive.

What's wrong with letting a user play with a user interface a bit to learn what it does?

Could someone who's never seen a car, but understands its general purpose, walk up to one and start driving? Some trial and error would probably be essential.

Of course, with software user interfaces we've trained users that the consequences of a misstep are almost as bad as they would be making the wrong choice in a car. Isn't that our fault for making unforgiving software that punishes the user for trying things out?

Making intuitive software means making software that works the way a user would expect. It doesn't mean that the user can instantly parse a user interface without pressing any buttons and know exactly how it works in detail. Software is expected to help us perform complex tasks. And sometimes it takes time for users to get "comfortable behind the wheel".

And that's okay.

Done right our software should be explorable. And pressing the wrong button shouldn't result in a fender bender (or worse).

CHAPTER SIXTEEN

Perfect is the enemy of the good (or great).

There have been countless blog posts on how trying to make something perfect usually ends up not only with nothing perfect, but often with nothing at all. This "common sense" is not so common. This precept is illustrated so well in this story from one of our favorite books "Art & Fear: Observations On the Perils (and Rewards) of Artmaking Paperback" by David Bayles and Ted Orland. Go out and buy several copies right now.

> "The ceramics teacher announced on opening day that he was dividing the class into two groups. All those on the left side of the studio, he said, would be graded solely on the quantity of work they produced, all those on the right solely on its quality. His procedure was simple: on the final day of class he would bring in his bathroom scales and weigh the work of the "quantity" group: fifty pound of pots rated an "A", forty pounds a "B", and so on. Those being graded on "quality", however, needed to produce only one pot — albeit a perfect one — to get an "A".

> Well, came grading time and a curious fact emerged: the works of highest quality were all produced by the group being graded for quantity. It seems that while the "quantity" group was busily churning out piles of work – and learning from their mistakes — the "quality" group had sat theorizing about perfection, and in the end had little more to show for their efforts than grandiose theories and a pile of dead clay."

Out of respect for the innocent, we'll refrain from naming the projects we've worked on that died on the vine of theoretical perfection. Suffice to say, there have been several.

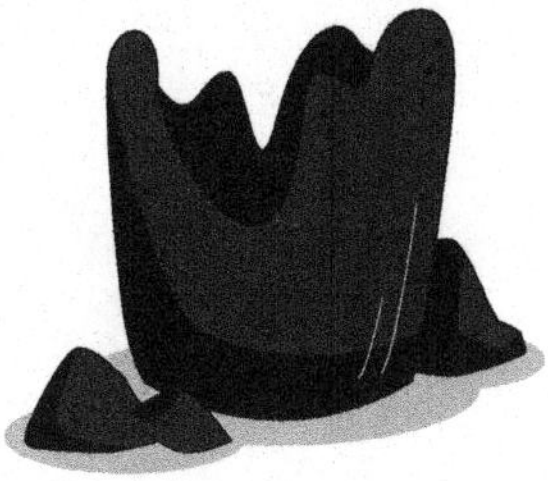

CHAPTER SEVENTEEN

The "First Impression" Quandary

"You never get a second chance to make a first impression" or so they say.

And when you're designing a piece of software, this is certainly true. If you turn customers off of your product with a lousy first experience, it doesn't matter how great the ongoing experience is as they'll never have it.

As an industry, we've over-optimized for our conscientiousness about making a good first impression in software. In other words, we're spending way too much time on first impressions, sometimes at the expense of the rest of the experience.

While this doesn't necessarily manifest itself in specific negative user interface trends, we do think it's a question of how much of your user experience cycles you spend on what part of your product. So many hours are spent usability testing a first experience, designing special introductions for a first experience, writing help topics for people learning how to use the product. It's not clear to us that this time is spent effectively. And we believe that this time is better spent on the long term user model and interface.

Here are two examples products where it appears the bulk of design time is spent on the long term experience:

Not all of us have the luxury of having products as singularly useful and dominant as a car… or Photoshop. Both are incredibly useful. Both own their market. And both are daunting to learn if you've never used them. Cars and Photoshop have terrible first experiences. They really do very little to get you up-to-speed gently with the product. Want to drive a car? Get lessons. Want to use Photoshop? Buy a book. And despite difficult first experiences, these products do quite well, and show no signs of spending a lot of time optimizing around their first experience.

Why?

As important as a first impression is, for products that are used every day like cars and Photoshop, the first impression becomes a progressively smaller percentage of the user's time spent with the product. On the second use it's 50%. On the fourth it's 25%. And over the lifetime of a typical user's relationship with one of these projects that first time calculated as a percentage of overall use becomes infinitesimal.

And yet, for many products, that are intended to be used every day, user experience professionals spend 90% of their time optimizing the design for that first impression. Usability tests are often designed to test users first experiences with the product (and often budgeted so that's as far as they typically go). These companies have spent the bulk of their user experience expertise focusing on a progressively smaller chunk of the user's overall experience with their product. Not the most thoughtful way to spend those resources.

And yet...

There are products however where the first impression is the daily impression. This is true in products that are used casually. Two good examples are 1) a drill, and 2) your bank's bill pay website. Typical users relearn how these services work every time they use them. Not because the users can't handle the complexity of the products (which aren't typically that hard to use in the first place). And not because they're lazy. But because users have plenty on their minds. And frankly, remembering how to add a new payee, or how to change a drillbit are just not worth the energy it takes to remember them. They'd rather relearn this information every time. For those of us who design software it may seem inefficient. But for most users, it's the most economical way to proceed. For these products, you will get a second chance to make a first impression. And a third and a fourth as well. And because of this, once again, in fact you're designing your product for every day use.

First impressions do count. It's critical to understand the role your product plays in your target audience's lives and then understand how to optimize from there.

CHAPTER EIGHTEEN

A Word on User Testing

Alright, more than a word.

You may have noticed that the title of this book is The Art of User Experience Design as opposed to The Science of User Experience Design. There's a reason for that. But first, some context.

The technology industry is populated overwhelmingly by engineers and business focused folks. Both groups love to measure things. They love cleanliness (despite what you may find in the engineers' offices). For the business folks, it's the bottom line. They can point to it. It doesn't lie. It simplifies things. *Did we get an ROI on this or not?*

For engineers, it's a little more subtle. For many of them it's an obsession with architectural beauty. After all, these people build things for a living and most of them take pride not just in the visible portions, but the beauty of what's inside their creation. And with good reason. But even more than that, many engineers subscribe to the notion that technology can solve most problems. It makes sense, as they are masters of technology. If technology has the power to solve most problems, then they themselves are gods (or at least god-like).

And in an age where technology really is solving many real problems, what's not to love? Twitter helps revolutions form. Uber shatters the taxicab monopoly of lousy customer service. Facebook connects you with long lost family. Technology is pretty amazing.

And when it comes to user experience, shouldn't we use some of the principles around making our code better to make our user interface better? The answer of course is, yes. Unfortunately for many executives and engineers, "test it with users" is the end of the conversation about whether a user experience design is any good, and in reality, that's just not going to work. Let's review a few techniques.

Personas

For years, user experience experts have advocated coming up with detailed profiles of fake real people that match the target audience for your product, or the existing audience depending on your situation. Knowing your customer is a good thing. So what's wrong with personas? Nothing per se. The problems are more in the weight personas are given, and how and when they are used.

If you are shipping a v1 of your product, you can know who you are targeting (in a broad sense) but you can't know who may respond to your product unexpectedly. Locking into one set of personas can be limiting in terms of opening your mind to new possibilities of audiences who might respond favorably to your software.

But more importantly, personas are never objective measures. By definition, they are simplifications of a broad and diverse audience that you may or may not truly understand. They minimize texture so you can get a handle on a broad group of people. And as such, they really don't represent anyone that well. Additionally, they are subject to the biases of both the folks that created the persona, and the folks that are interpreting the persona to make decisions.

What gives us pause is not the creation or use of personas, which is usually well-intentioned. What is difficult is when people proffer a persona as an evidence based argument for doing something one way or another. A persona is an opinion. It may have some data behind it, but it's not science.

User Testing During the Development Process

There are certainly learnings to be found from putting prototypes or alpha or beta versions of software in front of users before it's complete. They can find hard to understand user interface elements, get lost in the flow, and give you their gut reaction. With the right context, these are nice little hints as to where you can polish your experience.

However, user testing in this early part of the software development process will not give you a guarantee of creating a quality product that resonates with users. And unfortunately, many software teams today think that's the case. Why is this so?

The first hurdle you need to get through in order to have a successful software product is to actually get people to use your product. This is one of the hardest things to do. But by finding people and paying them to use your product you've already poisoned the testing pool. Your test users are not coming to use your product because they want to, they're using it because you made/paid them. Their entire motivation is suspect, and therefore so are their findings.

There are situations where companies have big installed bases and then beta test their latest software with a limited set of existing users of the old version of the product. This is a much more fruitful approach to user testing as these are your likely users. But in this case it's important to remember, that you are asking your most hardcore users to nitpick about changes you made that they will almost invariably complain about. Users don't like change. They often equate "easy" with "what they know". They may even like that your user interface is difficult because now that they've mastered it, it gives them a sense of superiority. It's really important to take this feedback with a grain of salt, and understand where it fits into the factors to which you should pay attention.

But most importantly, when it comes to user testing your unreleased software, odds are that your testers are treating this for what it is, a test. They're not necessarily using their real data in their natural environments. For software that affects mission critical data, they'd be crazy to run your beta software in a situation they actually needed to do their job. What if it broke? What if it corrupted their file? What if what if?

And finally, especially when testing software with new users, it's invariably their first experience. First impressions count, but they're a progressively smaller percentage of the user's time with the software as they use it. So optimizing all our efforts to take user feedback into account primarily around a user's first hour with our software seems like a misapplication of resources (see Chapter 18).

User Testing in the Wild

The perfect user test is the one where you ship a final version of your production software to a subset of your customer base and/or a subset of new customers coming to your product. You get to cordon off a number of your users in a controlled test and experiment on them in the real world. It means that you need to make sure this experimental flavor of your product won't harm them, and as a bonus, you should build in feedback mechanisms so they can let you know what they think. But the extra work is worth it because now you're testing real users in their real environments, who decided to use your product in a real way.

Qualitative Feedback

While we're not big fans of focus groups and the like, we have found one mechanism that is a pretty reliable indicator of where your users are struggling – your help system. For a user to be frustrated enough to call or email or post a problem, means that a) they really want to use your product, and b) they're willing to spend energy on getting around whatever problem they're having with it.

If you have enough support calls, you can start to get a sense of what matters and what doesn't The more calls and e-mails, the bigger problem you have.

Quantitative Feedback

With the advent of the web and analytics, measuring how users actually behave in your software as opposed to how they say they behave or how they behaved in an artificial lab setting is widespread. It's the darling of those engineers and business folks because it's incontrovertible. They love a good bottom line.

One of the best ways to use analytics is around encouraging users to make a purchase and comparing two candidates for a purchase page. Each has a slightly different design, and you're able to see which audience converted better. Of course it's imperative to make sure that as many other differentiating factors are eliminated and to have a statistically significant dataset.

But this can be overdone. There is the great story from a designer that quit Google who talked about A/B testing 41 different shades of blue. Why not 42? Maybe that 42nd shade would have been the winner? Snarkiness aside, the first question it's important to ask is, should the shade of blue make a difference?

There could be contrast considerations. There could be cultural considerations. So perhaps there are better and worse shades. But there are also time and resource considerations, not to mention ignoring expertise.

Choosing colors is not a fanciful exercise that anyone can do. Colors have meaning. Colors have relationships with other colors. And good user experience designers are trained in color theory.

Choosing the right colors is not always something you can defend with quantitative data analysis. That doesn't mean it's random.

And this is where the world of the designer and the world of the "just test it" crowd can conflict. User testing has a role, and an important one. Especially when the software is shipping. But user testing is not a crutch that obviates the need for software creators to have opinions.

The process of creating great software is an iterative one where with each loop the team uses user testing, both passive and active, to refine their own vision of the product. User testing can never answer 100% of the questions, so there will always be the need for leadership that's got a cohesive vision of the product that's being created. When that leadership uses user tests in just the right quantity to inform their own opinions and guide them, software improves, and teams reach their destination of satisfying users. When that leadership thinks that user testing is the final word on user experience design, in our experience, the ship ends up rudderless and meandering.

CHAPTER NINETEEN

More software is coming — whether we like it or not.

Every new idea in the modern world, every new initiative, just about every effort, public or private, personal or business-related, includes some form of digital expression. Software is the medium for that digital expression. Today, software is everywhere, whether we know it or not. Not just on our computers, our tablets, our phones, and our gaming devices (which could all be the very same object) but in our cars, in traffic lights, and in our thermostats. And in the future, this pervasiveness will only increase — dramatically. Imagine a world where every surface (and plane) is a potential display. Software is the primary language of the digital world we are creating.

Whether it's a birthday party requiring invitations, selling a house and advertising it on a web page, a new business, a new non-profit, a new curriculum from a third grade teacher, they all generate a need for digital expression. And that digital expression is more often than not sloppy, unfriendly, dumb, and in many cases... insulting. Whether the person with the idea is writing new software from scratch or using existing software to create a digital experience is irrelevant. The time we spend interacting with these creations is only going to increase. And the need for modern and talented technologists and software designers who share a holistic perspective on making these experiences positive has never been greater.

Software is the ubiquitous and universal medium that blankets our exponentially expanding digital world. More software is coming — whether we like it or not. The only question is whether any of it will be any good.

~~~

And now that you've read through our book, hopefully you are better prepared to deliver a positive answer to that question.
~~~

CHAPTER TWENTY

Everyone's a Designer

In the previous chapter we explained why the current plethora of software is nothing compared to the megatsunami on its way. Software will be like air, filling every available space and sensory "surface" in our lives.

The shortage of good developers and designers to make that software shows no signs of abating any time soon. But necessity is the mother of invention, and ironically, it will be software that solves this problem too.

Sooner rather than later, there will be software that lets everyone in effect become a software developer and de facto designer on their own. They won't need to learn to code, and they won't be reading these books. The tools they use to create new software will have a big influence on the output of their efforts.

Is this a good thing? We're not entirely sure how to answer that question. Let's just say, it's a thing.

More importantly, you can have a real impact on this future where everyone is designing the software we all use. You can set a great example. Every incremental inch of progress you make today, sets the bar higher for the next generation of user experiences.

Over and over again in today's software universe we see new concepts introduced. The ones that stick eventually get copied into all manner of applications. One of our favorites is the free throw user interface in basketball video games.

Originally, the user interface for throwing a free throw in a video game was, well, all over the place. The interface was random, and we're pretty sure in most cases that what the user did had almost no bearing on the result.

But then, one videogame had a crosshairs with a dot slowly moving horizontally across the crosshairs. The user would press the button when the dot was as close as possible to the center. And then the dot would navigate vertically, back and forth, like a cyborg's lone electronic eye and the user would repeat their behavior.

The closer the user got the two dots to the center of the crosshairs, the more likely the ball was to drop in the bucket. And of course, virtual players with better free throw shooting percentages got slower moving dots, while lousy free throw shooters had to contend with faster dots.

Other games saw this mechanism and copied it en masse. Some made minor improvements, but until today, that remains the essence of freethrow shooting in basketball videogames.

Just as these patterns are copied by professional user interface designers, they will be copied by the masses when they are designing their own software for their personal use. Your job is to set the bar as high as possible so the tools that let them join your ranks give them as much of an advantage as possible. Just think, someday, a pattern you created may be used in software all over the world.

THANK YOU!

TO OUR KICKSTARTER SUPPORTERS

Artefact
Vanessa Fox
Greg Storey
Christian Hagel
Scott Berkun
Natala Menezes
Peyman Oreizy
Deborah Dubrow
David D'Souza
Ray Palermo
Rachel Lanham
Sarah Bird
Sylvain Galineau
Alice Merchant
Stephen Dossick
Chris Evans
Marc Hedlund
Joseph Dickerson
Arlys Osborne
Amanda Powter
Jennifer Winters
paul jennings
Amir Koren
Deborah Hamel
Kevin Wong
Tom Berry
Ryan Schroeder
Adrian Klein
Adam Kinney
Si Daniels
Adam Phillabaum
Vinny Pasceri
Greg Pascale
Debra Weissman
Jerry Koh
Josh Santangelo
Kyle Kesterson
John
Evonne Benedict
Jennifer Sukis
Tom Kirby-Green
Azmir Saliefendic
Tom Tokarski
Michelle Goldberg
Kirill Zubovsky
Christen Coomer
inkblot
Matt Haughey
Bill Bliss
Anna Bevens
Marcelo Calbucci
Wendy Wolk Ryan
Kushal Chakrabarti
Paige Pauli
Tonya Engst
Narisa
Michele Freed
Brittany Staten
Ernest Lansford
Henry Rose
Eric Theriault
Keller Smith

Joel Stimson
Larry
Will Miceli
Ed Allard
Alex Hopmann
Greg Hochmuth
Jeff Ort
Linda Paton
Rich Schoenrock
Muness Castle
Ravi Chandrasekaran
Mark Bottomley
Rachel
Eric Nehrlich
Matt
Nate Miller
Paul Anguiano
Megan
Rebecca Lovell
Nishant Kothary
Mamie Rheingold
James Collins
Adam Doppelt
Rachel Doppelt
Aarron Walter
Doug Hanke
Nadja Haldimann
Michael Hart Leggett
Steven Glickman
Danielle Sheffler
Sarah Mackinnon

Chris Carter
Nick Grace
Matt Grommes
Kav Latiolais
Yoni Shechter
Jeremy Wemple
Jeff Whitmire
Amy Gorrek
David Sutoyo
Jan Molendijk
Dwight Battle
Tyesha
Ward Meremans
Jeff Boyus
Brittany
Bootstrapper Studios
Erwin Werkman
Kevin Lucca
Jonny McConnell
Cathie Toshach
Donovan
Josh Peters
Tommy Lewis
Dan Vogel
kaleemux
Cyriel van 't End
Brad Serbus
Andrew
Jamie Cabaccang
Kevin Davis

ACKNOWLEDGMENTS

When we first put our book up on Kickstarter, we had a particularly grand vision for it. Grand visions are good, but not when they get in the way of focus. The first outline for our book was all over the place. So we followed some of our own advice and simplified by breaking it into two books. The book in your hands is the second of those two books.

First and foremost our heartfelt thanks go to our hundreds of Kickstarter backers. They were incredibly patient, supportive, and helpful in getting the book out the door with quality. Thank you. We hope getting this second book is a nice treat for you.

Second, the team at Jackson Fish Market has been amazing as usual. The two of us founded JFM but the two of us don't make it work alone. Candy, John, Tom, and Kim are hard-working, creative, and a pleasure to work with. That last quality being the most important.

And of course, Tom in particular has brought his fresh, fun, and novel illustrative aesthetic to make both of these books what they are. His drawings convey the tone and message of the books and yet look like nothing you've ever seen on the shelf in the design and technology sections. We love that.

Scott Berkun's insightful and incisive editing gave our rambling opinions not just better form but better function. For that we are super grateful.

We are also so appreciative of the copy editing sweep that Adrian Klein gave the book. We love his attention to detail and appreciate the cheerleading he has given JFM over the years.

As designers in technology, we're part of a much larger community of bright and talented people. While this book represents our learnings, in many cases, our peers and colleagues are often our fellow students helping us learn, and in some cases, our teachers. Thank you for the inspiration.

We would be remiss if we didn't thank our amazing clients at Jackson Fish Market. The only way we can grow and learn the lessons we've tried to convey in these pages is by working with our customers and doing our best to understand each of their unique and important challenges. By letting us play a small role in helping to solve those design problems in their businesses, they've let us expand our knowledge, and now share it with you.

And of course, thank you to our friends and family who've been consistent and generous with their support and encouragement. We do our best every day to make them proud. We hope we've succeeded with this latest effort.

Hillel & Jenny

Made in the USA
Monee, IL
04 November 2026

67380169R00069